Medieval Welsh Literature to c.1400, including Arthurian Studies

A personal guide to
University of Wales Press publications
by

RACHEL BROMWICH

UNIVERSITY OF WALES PRESS
CARDIFF
1996

ISBN 0-7083-1376-0

Typeset in Cardiff at the University of Wales Press
Printed in Wales by Gwasg Dinefwr, Llandybïe
Cover design by John Garland, Pentan, Cardiff

Preface

Dr Rachel Bromwich was invited to prepare this booklet for the University of Wales Press and the Board of Celtic Studies of the University of Wales, with two audiences in mind.

Those already closely involved in medieval Welsh studies will surely appreciate a guide to the field written by one who is known to them as the editor of *Trioedd Ynys Prydain*, and the author of key studies in early Welsh literature, the Arthurian legend, and Dafydd ap Gwilym. But we have also become aware of a wider audience for our books among medievalists whose main interests are not Welsh or even Celtic, but who come to Welsh literature from a wider comparative perspective. Dr Bromwich is an ideal presenter of the material to this audience too. Her life has been spent between Cambridge (England) and Wales, between the Welsh and English languages, translating texts and interpreting the literature.

What follows is Dr Bromwich's own selection of and commentary on University of Wales Press titles that deal with Welsh literature to *c.*1400 – texts, critical studies and background reading. Most of the titles discussed are in print, but information regarding availability should be sought before placing an order (see p.50 for further details).

Ned Thomas
Director, University of Wales Press

Contents

Introduction

Almost a hundred years ago the essential foundations – linguistic, literary and historical – were laid for the renaissance in medieval Welsh studies which marked the earlier decades of the twentieth century. Of major significance was the work of the expert palaeographer Dr J. Gwenogvryn Evans (1852–1920) who, between 1907 and 1911 printed and published facsimiles and diplomatic editions of the thirteenth- and fourteenth-century manuscripts which contain nearly all of the oldest Welsh prose and poetry – the Black Book of Carmarthen, the 'White Book' Mabinogion, the Books of Aneirin and Taliesin, the Chirk Codex of the Welsh Laws, the Poetry from the Red Book of Hergest. The *Series of Old Welsh Texts* which he produced, alone and unaided, on his small hand-press at Pwllheli and later at Llanbedrog, followed the earlier reproductions and facsimiles on which he had collaborated with Sir John Rhŷs at Oxford, and which were published there: *The Mabinogion from the Red Book of Hergest* (1887), the *Facsimile of the Black Book of Carmarthen* (1888), *The Text of the Bruts from the Red Book of Hergest* (1890) and the *Book of Llandâf* (1893). Evans's works have rightly been called 'milestones in the history of publishing in Wales'; in the words of Sir John Morris-Jones 'for the first time they supplied Welsh scholars with reliable texts to work upon'. Evans's reproductions laid a secure basis for the exact scholarship of the succeeding generation, and his diplomatic editions have never been superseded. Hardly less important was his *Report on Manuscripts in the Welsh Language* which was produced in eight parts for the Historical Manuscripts Commission (London, 1898–1910); a catalogue whose extensive survey made it possible to locate Welsh manuscripts wherever they were to be found in the libraries of Wales or England, and which gave also a description of their content and an estimate as to their date. This work, too, has never been replaced, although its findings have occasionally been modified in the light of more recent scholarship. No less significant for the development of Welsh scholarship was the foundation in 1919 of the University's Board of Celtic Studies, with its **Bulletin**, whose first number was published in October 1921. One name stands out above all others in relation to these two major events, and that is the name of Ifor Williams (1881–1965, 'Sir Ifor' from 1947). Sir Ifor's scholarly editions of early Welsh poetry and of the Four Branches of the Mabinogi remain canonical texts to this day, and will long remain so; they are constantly reissued by the University of Wales Press to meet the needs of university teaching in successive generations, as well as to meet the wider needs of scholarship. More than any other individual, Sir Ifor was responsible for initiating the **Bulletin of the Board of Celtic Studies** (from 1995 it has been combined with **Studia Celtica**). From the beginning, Sir Ifor edited the Language and Literature section of the **Bulletin**, and for many years he was the main contributor to this section: from 1937 he was for ten years also the **Bulletin**'s general editor. Sir Ifor said that he was more proud of his 'Tarw Bach' (as he called it) than of any of the other publications with which he had been concerned; and this, he said, was because of the inspiration which the **Bulletin** had given, particularly to younger scholars, to make available to others the fruits of research without avoidable delay. Against all established tradition, and in the face of some initial opposition, Sir Ifor used Welsh for his lexicographical notes, and for almost everything else which he wrote for the **Bulletin** – just as he had broken with tradition by progressively employing Welsh in his lectures and classes. And it will be seen from this publication that Welsh was the language of all Sir Ifor's major publications 'megis ag y dylai ac y gweddai', as he expressed it. Yet no one would deny that Sir Ifor could be quite as relaxed, fluent and expressive a writer and a lecturer in English as he was in Welsh. This was well exemplified in the lectures and essays which are collected in **The Beginnings of Welsh Poetry** (p.5 below), as also in his *Dublin Lectures on Early Welsh Poetry* (Dublin Institute for Advanced Studies, 1944).

Y Cynfeirdd: Early Poets and Poetry

Editions and Studies

◆ Ifor Williams, **Canu Llywarch Hen** (1935, 1990). An edition
and discussion of the early three-line 'englynion' ('englynion o'r
hen ganiad') preserved in the Red Book of Hergest and in the
Black Book of Carmarthen. These poems relate to lost stories
concerning the figures of Llywarch Hen, Heledd and Urien
Rheged. They have as their background the wars between the
Cymry and the English in the sixth and seventh centuries, in
Powys and on the Shropshire border; but they also include
memories of warfare in the 'Old North' (the 'lost' territory which
covered much of southern Scotland, north-west England and the
Lake District). IW showed that, contrary to earlier assumption,
Llywarch Hen is not the name of the anonymous poet who
composed these dramatic poems, but rather that of a leading actor
in them, an ancient warrior who is depicted as a senile figure,
goading his sons to go out and fight in defence of their
borderland, as he himself is no longer able to do. IW gave an
outline of his theories in his British Academy Lecture of 1932
'The Poems of Llywarch Hen' which is reproduced as chapter viii
of **The Beginnings of Welsh Poetry** (p.5 below). It was primarily
on historical grounds that IW believed that the poems date from
the ninth century. [For translations and subsequent discussion of
all problems relating to these poems see Jenny Rowland, *Early
Welsh Saga Poetry* (D.S. Brewer, Woodbridge, 1990).]

◆ Ifor Williams, **Canu Aneirin** (1938, 1989). This is IW's
magnum opus. Many years of work lay behind his interpretation of
the obscure and archaic language of Aneirin's 'Gododdin'. He
recognized that the poem did not represent a new beginning, but
that underlying its linguistic and metrical complexities was a long
and largely obliterated poetic tradition. Traditionally, the

'Gododdin' was believed to have been composed by the poet
Aneirin at about the turn of the seventh century: the name is
derived from that of the British tribe of the Gododdin (Ptolemy's
'Votadini'), which had from the earliest times been settled in the
district of Lothian in south-east Scotland, perhaps with their
capital on the fortress-rock of Edinburgh. The poem is a series of
elegies on the young warriors (each one of them is individually
named) who set out from their homes to oppose a much larger
Anglian force from the south, at a place which is called Catraeth.
IW conjecturally identified Catraeth with Catterick in Yorkshire,
though he admitted that no absolute certainty as to the site can be
possible. Catterick was an important strategic position whose
possession would have been equally desirable to both Angles and
Britons, since it stood at the junction of Roman roads going to
the south as well as to the north-east and to the north-west.
Largely on the basis of converging historical evidence, IW
proposed that the Battle of Catraeth took place about the year
600, and was a disastrous failed attempt by the Britons to regain
possession of the site. But in the absence of any other contemporary reference to the battle outside the poem itself, all
details as to time and place remain of necessity hypothetical. Both
have subsequently been matters of much conjecture and
discussion; more recently, there has been increasing speculation
concerning the constituent elements of the text. [English
translations have been published by K.H. Jackson, *The Gododdin:
the Oldest Scottish Poem* (Edinburgh, 1969) and by A.O.H. Jarman,
Aneirin: Y Gododdin, with modernized Welsh text, full notes and a
glossary (Llandysul, 1988). See also Ifor Williams, **The Beginnings
of Welsh Poetry** (p.5 below), chapters iv, v and vi.]

◆ Ifor Williams, **Canu Taliesin** (1960, 1977, 1990). In the mixed
contents of the Book of Taliesin a nucleus of very early praise-
poems attributed to the sixth-century poet Taliesin had previously
been identified by John Morris-Jones (*Y Cymmrodor*, 28 (1918)).
IW conjectured that twelve of these were the authentic work of
the poet. They are here edited with introduction and notes. The
poems are addressed to the northern ruler Urien Rheged, to his
contemporary Gwallawg (who may have ruled in the Yorkshire
region of Elmet), to Urien's son Owain ab Urien, and one (of
uncertain authorship, but perhaps the earliest surviving poem in

4

Welsh) to Cynan Garwyn, a contemporary ruler of Powys. [English translation by J.E. Caerwyn Williams, *The Poems of Taliesin* (Dublin Institute for Advanced Studies, 1968).]

◆ Ifor Williams, **Armes Prydein o Lyfr Taliesin. Gyda Rhagymadrodd a Nodiadau** (1955, 1979). A tenth-century poem of political prophecy, which a later age erroneously attributed to Taliesin. IW concluded that 'Armes Prydein' was composed by a south-Wales ecclesiastic who wished to unite the peoples of Wales with those of Cornwall, Ireland, Strathclyde, Brittany and the Danes of Dublin, in order that – under the banner of St David – they might oppose the rising and oppressive power of the English king Athelstan (who is not actually named, however), and drive the English from Britain, thus restoring the sovereignty of the island to its original inhabitants. IW argues that the poem could not have been composed after the year 937, in which a comparable coalition of Britons, Scots and Danes of Dublin met with a crushing defeat at the hands of Athelstan at the Battle of Brunanburh. [English translation of IW's text and notes, by R. Bromwich, *Armes Prydein: the Prophecy of Britain* (Dublin Institute for Advanced Studies, 1972).] The literary context of 'Armes Prydein' – and of the cult of political prophecy in verse which developed from this time until resolved by the supposed triumph of the Britons at the Battle of Bosworth (1485) – was usefully outlined by M.E. Griffiths in **Early Vaticination in Welsh with English Parallels** (1937).

◆ Ifor Williams (ed. R. Bromwich), **The Beginnings of Welsh Poetry: Studies by Sir Ifor Williams, D. Litt., LL.D., FBA** (1972; 2nd edn 1980; pb. 1990). A reproduction of eight English articles and lectures by IW, including 'The Earliest Poetry', 'The Poems of Llywarch Hen', 'Wales and the North', 'The Towyn Inscribed Stone' and his editions of 'Edmic Dinbych' and of the Anglesey poem to Aeddon. With an introduction and some added notes by the editor.

◆ K.H. Jackson (ed.), **Early Welsh Gnomic Poems** (1935, 1973). 'Gnomes' are described as 'sententious statements about universals', whether these relate to human or to natural phenomena, and they include proverbs. KHJ here edits sequences of 'englynion' of the oldest type, mainly from the Red Book of Hergest, in which gnomic statements are combined with lines of frequently perceptive nature description. This is the earliest nature poetry to be found in Welsh. [Translations and full discussion in K. Jackson, *Early Celtic Nature Poetry* (Cambridge, 1935).]

A.O.H. Jarman, **Llyfr Du Caerfyrddin. Gyda Rhagymadrodd, Nodiadau Testunol a Geirfa** (1982). An edition and rearrangement of the entire contents of the Black Book of Carmarthen, with introduction, notes and glossary. The introductory section on 'Y Llawysgrif' is contributed by E.D. Jones (former librarian of the National Library of Wales), and establishes that the manuscript was written at different dates from *c.*1250 onwards. 'Y Cynnwys' by AOHJ then analyses the contents from both literary and historical viewpoints.

◆ A.O.H. Jarman (gol.), **Ymddiddan Myrddin a Thaliesin** (1951; new edn 1967). An edition and discussion of the obscure and allusive opening poem in the Black Book of Carmarthen, in which prophecies are expressed in the form of a dialogue between the two traditional poets Myrddin and Taliesin. Myrddin foretells events yet to come, some of which are alluded to elsewhere in the traditions about Myrddin (Merlin). On linguistic and metrical grounds the editor proposes a date in the latter half of the eleventh century. [Jarman's own translation of this and other 'Myrddin' poems is to be found in an appendix to N. Tolstoy, *The Quest for Merlin* (London, 1983).]

◆ A.O.H. Jarman, **The Cynfeirdd: Early Welsh Poets and Poetry** ('Writers of Wales', 1981). A succinct account of the earliest poetry, developed largely from the pioneer interpretations of John Morris-Jones and Ifor Williams, but with several original comments on the varieties of expression given in Welsh to the heroic ethos. AOHJ discerns a contrast between Taliesin's seminal portrayal of Urien Rheged as an idealized ruler and the passionate quest for personal glory which motivates the young warriors of the 'Gododdin'. He describes the latter poem as 'the only complete expression of the heroic ideal in Welsh literature'. In the Llywarch Hen poetry he finds the 'anti-heroic' expression of this ideal.

◆ R. Bromwich and R. Brinley Jones (goln/eds), **Astudiaethau ar yr Hengerdd: Studies in Old Welsh Poetry. Presented to Sir Idris Foster** (1978). A collection of specialist studies (some in English and some in Welsh) by a number of contributors. Though concerned primarily with the 'Gododdin' poem – its historicity (T.M. Charles-Edwards), language (D. Simon Evans) and metrics (D. Ellis Evans) – it includes also editions of the poems and fragments concerning Cadwallon (R.G. Gruffydd), the 'Marwnad Cunedda' (J.E. Caerwyn Williams), the Llywarch Hen poetry (N.J.A. Williams and Gwyn Thomas) and the early dramatic and dialogue poems from the Black Book of Carmarthen (B.F. Roberts). (Two of these last poems are of primary interest for Arthurian studies.) An editorial introduction in English outlines the contents of the book.

Y Gogynfeirdd: The Poets of the Princes

Editions and Studies

◆ J. Morris-Jones and T.H. Parry-Williams (goln), **Llawysgrif Hendregadredd** (NLW MS 6880B) (1933, 1978). This edition of the oldest collection of the poetry of the Gogynfeirdd ('the not so early poets') completes the series inaugurated by J. Gwenogvryn Evans of diplomatic editions of important Welsh medieval manuscripts. Hendregadredd was written by various hands from *c.*1300 through the following century, and contains the work of named poets who composed between *c.*1100 and 1282, from Meilyr Brydydd to Bleddyn Fardd. On blank spaces there have been added extracts by a later generation of poets, including Gruffudd Gryg and Dafydd ap Gwilym. This is the only source for Dafydd ap Gwilym's early poem 'I'r Grog o Gaer', and it is possible that it was written here in his own hand. [Essential discussion is by Daniel Huws, 'Llawysgrif Hendregadredd' *Journal of the National Library of Wales* xxii (1981), 1–26.]

◆ R.G. Gruffydd (gol. cyff.) **Cyfres Beirdd y Tywysogion** (Series of the Poets of the Princes) (7 vols, 1991–6). A collection of eulogistic and religious poetry, addressed to their patrons, to God, or to one or other of the Welsh saints, by the official poets attached to the Welsh princes during the period of independence from *c.*1100 to the Edwardian Conquest of 1282. The work of each of the poets is edited separately by a different scholar, with a separate introduction to each poem, which discusses its date, historical background, metre and manuscript sources: these are mainly from H (Hendregadredd) or RBP (Poetry from the Red Book of Hergest), but a stemma is given indicating any later copies. The edited poem follows, first in its original form, then in modernized spelling, and finally by a modern paraphrase, with notes, glossary and an index of names and places. The **Cyfres** provides an unprecedented comprehensive edition of the bardic poetry of the last two centuries of Welsh independence. Editing has been the work of a team of scholars employed during a six-year period by the Canolfan Uwchefrydiau Cymreig a Cheltaidd/Centre for Advanced Welsh and Celtic Studies at Aberystwyth. The seven volumes are: I: **Gwaith Meilyr Brydydd a'i ddisgynyddion, ynghyd â dwy awdl fawl ddienw o Ddeheubarth** (Meilyr Brydydd and his Descendants, with two anonymous early twelfth-century 'awdlau') (1994); II: **Gwaith Llywelyn Fardd I ac eraill o feirdd y ddeuddegfed ganrif** (Llywelyn Fardd I and other twelfth-century poets) (1994); III: **Gwaith Cynddelw Brydydd Mawr I** (1991); IV: **Gwaith Cynddelw Brydydd Mawr II** (1995); V: **Gwaith Llywarch ap Llywelyn 'Prydydd y Moch'** (1991); VI: **Gwaith Dafydd Benfras ac eraill o feirdd hanner cyntaf y drydedd ganrif ar ddeg** (Dafydd Benfras and other poets of the first half of the thirteenth century) (1995); VII: **Gwaith Bleddyn Fardd a beirdd eraill ail hanner y drydedd ganrif ar ddeg** (Bleddyn Fardd and other poets of the second half of the thirteenth century) (1996).

◆ H. Lewis (gol.), **Hen Gerddi Crefyddol** (Early Religious Poems) (1931, 1974). A collection of religious verse, with introduction, notes and glossary. The early (anonymous) poems are from the Black Book of Carmarthen and the Book of Taliesin; the Gogynfeirdd poems are from the Hendregadredd manuscript and the Red Book of Hergest; some variants from later manuscripts are noted. Texts are reproduced with the minimum of alteration, but line-division and punctuation are supplied.

◆ M.E. Owen and B.F. Roberts (goln), **Beirdd a Thywysogion** (Poets and Princes) (1996). A collection of studies concerning the poetry of the Gogynfeirdd, by friends, pupils and colleagues, presented to Professor R. Geraint Gruffydd on his retirement, and concerning various aspects of the panegyric and religious verse composed by the Poets of the Princes to their patrons in the period c.1100–1282. With contributions on bardic poetry from Irish and Gaelic sources.

◆ J.E. Caerwyn Williams, **The Poets of the Welsh Princes** ('Writers of Wales', 1978; new edn 1994). JECW outlines the characteristics of twelfth- and thirteenth-century court poetry – 'mawl', 'marwnad', 'gorhoffedd', 'rhieingerdd' etc. He stresses the continuity of the Gogynfeirdd from the Cynfeirdd in vocabulary and technique, as well as their earlier inheritance from the bards and druids of Britain and Gaul. The Gogynfeirdd aimed to recreate in their work the essential character of the poetry of their predecessors, and on occasion they repeated identifiable lines from Aneirin and Taliesin. The ancient heroic ethos survived the transition to Christianity. Contemporary evidence from the Welsh Laws as to the status and functions of the 'pencerdd' and 'bardd teulu' is cited. The revised edition ends with a useful list of the poets' names, together with the names of the princes whom they addressed, and has a select bibliography.

◆ D. Myrddin Lloyd, **Rhai Agweddau ar Ddysg y Gogynfeirdd** (Darlith Goffa G.J. Williams, 1977). An analysis of the references made by the Poets of the Princes to the traditional heroes of Wales, whether these were known to them by oral tradition, from the genealogies of the rulers of Gwynedd, Powys and Deheubarth, or were characters derived from the 'Trioedd' and 'chwedlau'. After 1282 the poets' field of reference widened considerably to include the heroes and heroines known from the romances, both Welsh and foreign.

◆ D. Simon Evans, **Medieval Religious Literature** ('Writers of Wales', 1986). DSE shows how from the beginning the Christian religion was blended with the native culture, and how in Wales the theme of praise remained as dominant in religious as in secular poetry. The book outlines the variety of religious themes to be found in the verse of the Gogynfeirdd and their successors the Cywyddwyr, such as the Signs before Domesday, the Dispute between Body and Soul, and the Harrowing of Hell. It is shown how the poetry of the Cywyddwyr reflects the alterations in religious attitudes which were brought about by the social and political changes which followed the Edwardian Conquest. The Lives of the Welsh Saints (Y Bucheddau) are also discussed, as are the increasing influences on poetry of foreign religious works.

[Generous selections from the poetry of the Cynfeirdd and the Gogynfeirdd are given in English translation by A. Conran, *The Penguin Book of Welsh Verse* (1967; revised edn *Welsh Verse* (Bridgend, 1986), and by J.P. Clancy, *The Earliest Welsh Poetry* (London, 1970) and *Medieval Welsh Lyrics* (London, 1965).]

Y Cywyddwyr Cyntaf:
Fourteenth-Century Poets and Poetry

◆ Ifor Williams and Thomas Roberts, **Cywyddau Dafydd ap Gwilym a'i Gyfoeswyr** (goln) (Poems of Dafydd ap Gwilym and his Contemporaries) (1935; a revised edn of a work originally printed by E. Thomas, Bangor, 1914). This edition of selected poems attributed to Dafydd ap Gwilym and to his four contemporaries Gruffudd Gryg, Gruffudd ab Adda, Madog Benfras and Llywelyn Goch ap Meurig Hen, is based on the collation of a number of manuscripts. It is introduced by an abbreviated form of IW's extended essay 'Dafydd ap Gwilym a'r Glêr' (*Transactions of the Honourable Society of Cymmrodorion* 1913–14) – a study which strongly influenced all subsequent discussions of the European influences on Dafydd ap Gwilym's poetry. Besides poems by the poet's contemporaries, **Cywyddau Dafydd ap Gwilym a'i Gyfoeswyr** includes some twenty poems from the *editio princeps* – *Barddoniaeth Dafydd ap Gwilym* (eds Owen Jones and W. Owen Pughe, London, 1789), all of which were subsequently rejected by Thomas Parry, as of doubtful authenticity, from his canon of the poet's work, as established by him in **Gwaith Dafydd ap Gwilym** (see pp.12–13 below). Nevertheless, **Cywyddau Dafydd ap Gwilym a'i Gyfoeswyr** remains essential for study, not least for its introductory essay and notes. (T.M. Chotzen's *Recherches sur la Poésie de Dafydd ap Gwilym* (Amsterdam, 1927) was largely inspired by IW's essay of THSC 1914, but IW was in turn influenced in his revised introduction to the 1935 edition of **Cywyddau Dafydd ap Gwilym a'i Gyfoeswyr** by Chotzen's citations of further European parallels.) [For some of the work of Dafydd's contemporary poets see D. Johnston, *Blodeugerdd Barddas o'r Bedwaredd Ganrif ar Ddeg* (Llandybie, 1989).]

11

◆ Ifor Williams, Henry Lewis and Thomas Roberts, **Cywyddau Iolo Goch ac Eraill** (goln) (1937, 1979). This is a revised edition of *Iolo Goch ac Eraill*, printed by Evan Thomas (Bangor, 1925), a collection of poems by poets *c*.1350–1450, with introduction, notes and glossary. This edition is now partly superseded by D. Johnston, **Gwaith Iolo Goch** (p.14 below). But **Cywyddau Iolo Goch ac Eraill** remains valuable as it contains the work of Iolo's contemporaries and successors – Gruffudd Llwyd, Ieuan ap Rhydderch, Siôn Cent, Rhys Goch Eryri, Llywelyn ab y Moel, Sypyn Cyfeiliog, Iorwerth ab y Cyriog and Ieuan Waed Da, few of whose poems have as yet appeared in critical editions. An introduction discusses the work of these poets. For Gruffudd Llwyd see now D. Johnston, op. cit. in previous note, and Saunders Lewis, **Braslun o Hanes Llenyddiaeth Gymraeg** (pp.16–17 below, chapter vi).

◆ Thomas Parry (gol.), **Gwaith Dafydd ap Gwilym** (1952; revised edn 1963; pb. 1996). This edition seeks to establish by modern standards an authentic canon for the poetry attributed over the centuries to Dafydd ap Gwilym (*c*.1315–20 to 1350–70), the foremost poet of medieval Wales, and a major European poet. There is a full critical apparatus, with introduction, notes and glossary. The book is based on some twenty years' study by the editor of the variant manuscript versions of nearly 300 poems, all of which were previously claimed to be the work of Dafydd ap Gwilym. Parry reduced to some 150 the 262 poems attributed to the poet in the *editio princeps*, *Barddoniaeth Dafydd ap Gwilym* (eds Owen Jones and William Owen Pughe, London, 1789). In his introduction Parry outlines the few details which can be deduced concerning the poet's life, with all the information which is available concerning the various men and women to whom Dafydd addressed his poems, or who are alluded to in them. Parry sets forth clearly the metrical and linguistic criteria on which he based his decisions as to authenticity, while he admits that absolute certainty on this is not possible in every single case. The text is based on a full collation of the manuscripts: variant readings are listed, but the choice between contradictory forms among these has been made by the editor. Spelling and punctuation have been modernized. The 1963 edition of **Gwaith Dafydd ap Gwilym** contains some brief but important additions to the notes, and some alterations to an abbreviated form of the earlier introduction. (Many readers will regret that this edition, and subsequent reprints of **Gwaith Dafydd ap Gwilym**, omit the valuable section on pp.clxx–cxc of the 1952 first edition, in which Parry gave brief notes on his reasons for rejecting the authenticity of each one of the 177 additional poems accepted as authentic by the editors of the 1789 *Barddoniaeth Dafydd ap Gwilym*.)

◆ R.M. Loomis, **Dafydd ap Gwilym: The Poems** (Binghamton, New York, 1982; distributed in Britain by the University of Wales Press). A prose translation of the complete canon of Dafydd ap Gwilym's verse, as defined and edited by Thomas Parry (see previous entry). A useful work for students, as the numbering of the poems corresponds with the numbers in **Gwaith Dafydd ap Gwilym**. [For selections from **Gwaith Dafydd ap Gwilym**, giving Parry's edited text with facing prose translations, new introduction and notes, see also R. Bromwich, *Dafydd ap Gwilym: A Selection of Poems* (in Gwasg Gomer's series, 'The Welsh Classics', Llandysul, 1982; new edn 1987, 1993; also Harmondsworth, 1987).]

◆ John Rowlands (gol.), **Dafydd ap Gwilym a Chanu Serch yr Oesau Canol** (Dafydd ap Gwilym and the Love-Poetry of the Middle Ages) (1975). Six lectures delivered at a colloquium held under this title at Gregynog in 1975: 'Serch Fabliau a Serch Cwrtais' (Peter Dronke); 'Serch Cwrtais mewn Llenyddiaeth Wyddeleg' (Séan Ó Tuama); 'Dafydd ap Gwilym: Y Traddodiad Islenyddol' (Rachel Bromwich); 'Cymru yn Oes Dafydd ap Gwilym' (Rees Davies); 'Dafydd ap Gwilym y Bardd' (Dafydd Elis Thomas); 'Rhai Agweddau ar Gywyddau Serch y Bymthegfed Ganrif' (Gilbert Ruddock). (The first three lectures are translated from English.)

◆ Rachel Bromwich, **Aspects of the Poetry of Dafydd ap Gwilym: Collected Papers** (1986). The six essays include the writer's booklet *Dafydd ap Gwilym*, first published in the 'Writers of Wales' series (1974); **Tradition and Innovation in the Poetry of Dafydd ap Gwilym** (1967, 1972); 'Dafydd ap Gwilym: the Sub-literary Tradition', 'Dafydd ap Gwilym and the Bardic Grammar', and an essay on the Welsh Cywyddwyr who were the poet's near contemporaries. The introduction compares Dafydd ap Gwilym's linguistic inheritance and historical circumstances with those of his contemporary Geoffrey Chaucer.

◆ Helen Fulton, **Dafydd ap Gwilym and the European Context** (1989). A study of the poet, in relation to his literary inheritance from both Wales and the European continent, and in the context of the changed sociological conditions in fourteenth-century Wales which resulted from the Edwardian Conquest of 1282.

◆ Dafydd Johnston (gol.), **Gwaith Iolo Goch** (1988). A definitive edition of thirty-nine poems accepted by the editor as the authentic work of the poet, with introduction, notes and glossary. Iolo Goch (*c*.1325–97?) was a junior contemporary of Dafydd ap Gwilym, whom he long outlived, and to whom he composed an elegy. Over the years, Iolo's reputation has tended to be overshadowed by that of Dafydd ap Gwilym, and this new edition goes far to adjust the balance. The text has been established from the collation of a number of manuscripts (many poems ascribed in the manuscripts to Iolo have been rejected as unauthentic). Iolo adapted the new 'cywydd' metre to the older and more formal poetic tradition of 'awdlau' addressed by the bards to their patrons. The patrons to whom he addressed 'cywyddau' included Sir Rhys ap Gruffudd, Sir Hywel ap Gruffudd and Owain Glyndŵr – men who were prominent not only in Welsh affairs, but had made their reputations also beyond the borders of Wales. Iolo evidently had some knowledge of English, and his concern with contemporary affairs is demonstrated in two adulatory poems, the one addressed to King Edward III, urging him to set forth on a crusade to the Holy Land, and the other to Sir Roger Mortimer, the heir apparent to the throne of Richard II, inciting him to savage acts of warfare in his earldom of Ulster. Iolo Goch had close relations with leading members of the Church, and a number of his poems appear to be intended primarily for an ecclesiastical audience. Among these is his famous poem to the abstract figure of the Ploughman, which echoes the intense feelings aroused among both lay and ecclesiastical landholders by the Peasants' Revolt of 1381. [Dafydd Johnston has subsequently published an extended essay on Iolo Goch for the series *Llên y Llenor* (Caernarfon, 1989). His English translation of Iolo's poems, with the text as in **Gwaith Iolo Goch** and with facing translations, is published in the 'Welsh Classics' series, *Iolo Goch: Poems* (Llandysul, 1993).]

◆ G.J. Williams and E.D. Jones (goln), **Gramadegau'r Penceirddiaid** (1934). A magistral introduction by G.J. Williams is followed by editions of three fourteenth-century texts of the Bardic Grammar (the 'dwned'), which are attributed either to Einion Offeiriad or to Dafydd Ddu Athro of Hiraddug. All derive from a common original of the thirteenth century believed to have been composed by a poet who may also have been a cleric. As a preliminary, the text outlines the science of (Latin) grammar as established by Donatus and Priscian, and follows this with an extended analysis of Welsh prosody, citing examples of the different types of 'awdl', 'englyn' and 'cywydd', and concluding with some re-adaptations of the Grammar by poets of the fifteenth and sixteenth centuries. **Gramadegau'r Penceirddiaid** is an essential work for understanding the techniques of medieval Welsh poetry, as well as for the light which it sheds on some fragmentary poetic sources which may have influenced Dafydd ap Gwilym. [See T. Parry, 'The Welsh Metrical Treatise attributed to Einion Offeiriad', *Proceedings of the British Academy* xlvii (1961), and R.G. Gruffydd, 'Wales's Second Grammarian, Dafydd Ddu of Hiraethog', PBA (1995).]

◆ Saunders Lewis, **Gramadegau'r Penceirddiaid** (Darlith Goffa G.J. Williams, 1967). An important, if controversial, discussion of the early texts of the Bardic Grammar. Saunders Lewis argues for the priority of the version which attributes the Grammar's composition to Dafydd Ddu of Hiraddug (Peniarth 20) over that which assigns it to Einion Offeiriad (Red Book of Hergest).

◆ B.F. Roberts (gol.), **Gwassanaeth Meir** (1961). This translation of the *Officium Parvum Beatae Mariae Virginis* or 'Little Office of the Blessed Virgin Mary' is the only surviving medieval Welsh translation of a part of the pre-Reformation Church services. It was made during the second half of the fourteenth century. A point of interest is that the translation is almost entirely rendered into verse, and into a combination of 'canu caeth' and 'canu rhydd' (the strict and the free metres), with very little accompanying prose. The poet is named in one manuscript as Dafydd Ddu Athro o Hiraddug (with whose name compare the two entries above). This attribution appears to have been traditional: if true, it would explain the poet's evidently greater familiarity with 'canu caeth' than with 'canu rhydd'.

Gwassanaeth Meir contains some of the earliest extant examples of 'canu rhydd'.

R.I. Daniel (gol.), **Ymborth yr Enaid** (Sustenance of the Soul) (1995). This text is unique in that it is an original devotional work, rather than a work translated from Latin, as were the other mystical and doctrinal treatises which accompany it in the fourteenth-century Llyfr Ancr Llanddewibrefi. Iestyn Daniel gives reasons to support his belief that the author of **Ymborth yr Enaid** was a thirteenth-century Dominican friar, who possessed a distinction of style and language which he had acquired from a preceding bardic training in the strict metres of Welsh poetry, as well as in the composition of prose. Particularly impressive is the friar's reported account of his vision of the child Jesus, in language which recalls the native 'araith' (oration, rhetoric). The editor relates **Ymborth yr Enaid** to the language of the Bardic Grammar, to **Gwassanaeth Meir**, and to the verse of the friar Madog ap Gwallter, and he makes some interesting suggestions as to the possibilities of common authorship. The text is edited with an introduction and notes.

◆ J. Morris-Jones, **Cerdd Dafod: sef Celfyddyd Barddoniaeth Gymraeg**. Reprinted with an index by Geraint Bowen in 1980, it was first published at Oxford in 1925. JMJ's *ars poetica* has long been established as the definitive authority on the rules governing the different types of 'cynghanedd' (harmony, alliteration) and metre as these were developed in Wales over a period of ten centuries. The writer's close familiarity with a wide range of manuscript sources enabled him to illustrate the varieties of 'awdl', 'cywydd' and 'englyn' by quotations from the work of poets from the earliest times to the late fifteenth century. For its stylistic qualities, no less than for its content, it has been said that **Cerdd Dafod** 'deserves to be ranked with the major [Welsh] prose-works of the [present] century'.

◆ Saunders Lewis, **Braslun o Hanes Llenyddiaeth Gymraeg: I. Hyd at 1535** (1932, 1986). This 'Outline of the History of Welsh Literature' was planned as the first volume of a work which remained unfinished. The foundation of the tradition of Welsh praise-poetry is traced to the encomiastic verses which the sixth-century Taliesin traditionally addressed to his patron Urien Rheged. Taliesin was considered by the Gogynfeirdd to be the founder and inspiration of their poetic art, and he was recognized as such by succeeding poets. The mutual relation between praise-poet and his noble patron was confirmed and matured in the teaching of the bards, and their teaching was incorporated into Einion Offeiriad's Bardic Grammar (p.15 above). Just as poetry was nurtured in the teaching of the bards, so it is claimed that it was from the teaching afforded in the early medieval law schools that the rich tradition of medieval Welsh prose literature was evolved. Although in some respects controversial, SL's essays in this book contain much stimulating literary and philosophical comment and criticism, and remain of great interest and value, although at times they require adjustment in the light of more recent scholarship. Many of his ideas were further developed in his later essays (p.47 below).

◆ Gwyn Thomas, **Y Traddodiad Barddol** (The Bardic Tradition) (1976, 1993). Though published nearly fifty years subsequently to it, this survey of Welsh poetry from the earliest times to the sixteenth century covers much of the same ground as Saunders Lewis's **Braslun** (to which the author frequently refers), but mirrors certain major advances in scholarship which have been made during the intervening period – particularly in relation to Ifor Williams's editions and studies of the early poetry, and to Thomas Parry's edition of the poems of Dafydd ap Gwilym. Gwyn Thomas emphasizes the original oral composition and transmission of the Welsh poetic tradition, and the fact that this was already ancient when it was inherited by Taliesin and the other Cynfeirdd. Afterwards it was passed down through predominantly oral channels, in the teaching given by the bards to their pupils. The book is written in. lively contemporary idiom, and though addressed primarily to students in school and college, it is probable that it will long continue to appeal to a much wider audience. Particularly welcome is the percipient discussion and commentary on the poetry of all periods, and the paraphrases given in clear modern prose to elucidate difficult passages of verse.

Cyfarwyddyd: Welsh Tales and Foreign Adaptations

Texts and Editions

J.G. Evans, and R.M. Jones, **Llyfr Gwyn Rhydderch: Y Chwedlau a'r Rhamantau** (The White Book of Rhydderch: Tales and Romances) (1972, 1977). A reprint of J.G. Evans's *White Book Mabinogion; Tales and Romances* (Pwllheli, 1907), with a new introduction by R.M. Jones. Together with much other material, the 'White Book' contains the oldest complete texts of ten of the eleven 'Mabinogion' tales (the eleventh, 'Breuddwyd Rhonabwy', is here supplied from the Red Book of Hergest). 'The White Book provides the earliest texts of much of the best of Welsh medieval secular prose . . . Only the Red Book of Hergest can be compared to it in importance' according to the estimate of Daniel Huws, 'Llyfr Gwyn Rhydderch', *Cambridge Medieval Celtic Studies* 21 (1991), 1–37. The same authority here concludes that the manuscript was written by five different scribes, all of them working *c*.1350.

♦ Ifor Williams, **Pedeir Keinc y Mabinogi** (The Four Branches of the Mabinogi) (1930; new edn 1951, 1994). More than sixty years since its first publication, IW's edition of the Mabinogi remains fundamental for the study of the four tales 'Pwyll Pendefig Dyfed', 'Branwen ferch Lŷr', 'Manawydan fab Llŷr' and 'Math fab Mathonwy'. IW here provided for the first time a satisfactory explanation of the title 'Mabinogi', as meaning 'youth, a tale of youth' and then simply 'a tale'. With W.J. Gruffydd (p.27 below) he regarded the south Wales hero Pryderi as the single central figure around whose life the composite Mabinogi could have developed. He suggested that the work was first redacted by a south Wales author during the brief period when the whole country was united under Gruffudd ap Llywelyn ap Seisyll (d. 1063), and that this author based his work on antecedent, orally preserved legend and mythology. Edited with introduction and copious explanatory notes. [English editions of 'Pwyll' and 'Branwen', by R.L. Thomson and D.S. Thomson respectively, and based on IW's edition, were published by the Dublin Institute for Advanced Studies in 1957, 1961. For English translations of the eleven tales see Gwyn Jones and Thomas Jones, *The Mabinogion* (Everyman, 1949) and J. Ganz, *The Mabinogion* (Harmondsworth, 1976).]

◆ Rachel Bromwich and D. Simon Evans, **Culhwch ac Olwen: Testun Syr Idris Foster, wedi ei olygu a'i orffen gan RB a DSE** (CO (i)) (1988). A revised edition of CO (i) is in the Press and is scheduled for publication in 1997. It will have full notes and critical apparatus, and a revised text edited from the White Book of Rhydderch and the Red Book of Hergest.

◆ Rachel Bromwich and D. Simon Evans, **Culhwch and Olwen: An Edition and Study of the Oldest Arthurian Tale** (CO (ii)) (1992). The text of the tale corresponds in the two editions, CO (i) and CO (ii), but CO (ii) offers a newly written introduction which acknowledges indebtedness to the earlier work of Sir Idris Foster, makes some new suggestions, and takes account of studies published after the death of Sir Idris in 1984.

With the Four Branches of the Mabinogi, 'Culhwch and Olwen' represents the oldest of the Welsh tales which has survived in a complete form. Like the Four Branches, it is the final redaction in writing of a long antecedent tradition of oral story-telling: a tradition which has left its influence in different ways on the style of both 'Culhwch and Olwen' and the Four Branches. (See P. Mac Cana, **The Mabinogi**, p.26 below.)

◆ Glenys W. Goetinck (gol.), **Historia Peredur vab Efrawc** (1976). Edited from the White Book of Rhydderch and the Red Book of Hergest. With brief introduction, notes, and glossary (in Welsh). (Fragmentary texts from Peniarth 7 and 14 are printed in an appendix.) Peredur was an ancient traditional hero of the 'Old North', whose name is found in the 'Gododdin'. (Efrawg < Eburācon = York). With 'Owein' and 'Geraint ab Erbin' this tale is known as one of the Three Romances in the 'Mabinogion'. The three tales are united in their similarity of style and subject-matter: the names of the protagonists in all three have close parallels in those of their counterparts in the corresponding poems of Chrétien de Troyes – 'Perceval li Gallois', 'Yvain', 'Erec et Enide'. In the Welsh version, Peredur's story contains within it the germ of the Grail legend, which was developed more explicitly by Chrétien de Troyes. See Goetinck's **Peredur: A Study of Welsh Tradition in the Grail Legends** (p.31 below).

Melville Richards, **Breudwyt Ronabwy** (The Dream of Rhonabwy) (1948, 1980). This tale is the latest to be included in the 'Mabinogion'. The only surviving text has been preserved in the Red Book of Hergest. 'Rhonabwy's Dream' may have been composed in the middle or later thirteenth century, and in character it contrasts strongly with all the other Welsh tales. A precise historical and geographical setting – Powys under the rule of Madog ap Maredudd (d.1160) – is sharply juxtaposed to the fantasy of an occult dream-vision, which discloses to Madog's messenger Rhonabwy the visionary panorama of Arthur's court, peopled with legendary heroes, all no doubt familiar names to the author, and to the reader or listener to the tale. Both the Arthurian world and the narrator's contemporary world are satirized concurrently, though at this distance of time it is impossible for us to estimate the finer points of the satire.

◆ Patrick K. Ford (ed.), **Ystoria Taliesin** (1992). The first scholarly edition, with an extended introduction, notes and glossary, of a folk-tale which is presumed to be of great antiquity, telling of the miraculous birth of the 'archetypal Celtic poet' Taliesin; of how he acquired the 'awen', or gift of poetic inspiration and prophecy, and was later enabled by this to confute an assembly of rival poets at the court of the king Maelgwn Gwynedd. The text is based on that of Elis Gruffydd, the sixteenth-century 'soldier of Calais' who acknowledges that in his day there existed many variant oral versions of the tale. [The story was first made known in English through T. Love Peacock's *The Misfortunes of Elphin* (1829), and subsequently a text and translation, from a version by Iolo Morganwg, was included in Lady Charlotte Guest's *Mabinogion* in 1849. See also Ifor Williams, **Chwedl Taliesin**, p.29 below).]

◆ Rachel Bromwich, **Trioedd Ynys Prydein: The Welsh Triads**. Edited with introduction, translation and commentary (1961; new edn 1978; 3rd edn in the Press and scheduled for publication in 1997). The 'Triads of the Island of Britain' are a series of triple groups commemorating the names of heroes and heroines from an extensive corpus of lost Welsh traditional narrative, which was for the most part only retailed orally, and hence has very largely been lost to posterity. But the traditional names are frequently recalled in tantalizing allusions by the Gogynfeirdd and later poets, as well as in the Mabinogi and elsewhere. The Triads have come down in numerous manuscript copies from the late thirteenth century onwards (though some individual triads are certainly much older than this). The names are grouped under various imprecise but complimentary epithets, often paralleled in the esoteric language of the poets. The book ends with five appendices: Bonedd Gwŷr y Gogledd (The Descent of the Men of the North); Tri Thlws ar Ddeg Ynys Prydein (The Thirteen Treasures of the Island of Britain), Enweu Ynys Prydein (The Names of the Island of Britain) and Pedwar Marchog ar Hugain Llys Arthur (The Twenty-Four Knights of Arthur's Court) and North Welsh Genealogical Triads.

◆ R. Bromwich, **Trioedd Ynys Prydain in Welsh Literature and Scholarship** (G.J. Williams Memorial Lecture, 1969). This lecture outlines the reverential attitude held towards Trioedd Ynys Prydain as a prime historical source from the time of the Renaissance scholars Salesbury and Camden, and culminating in Iolo Morganwg's compilation and publication of his 'Third Series' of Trioedd Ynys Prydain in the *Myvyrian Archaiology of Wales* in 1807. The basis of his work was an imaginative recreation of Triads from the older collection compiled by Robert Vaughan of Hengwrt (1592–1667; see triads 1–46 in the previous entry), and published as the *Myvyrian* 'First Series' of Trioedd Ynys Prydain. [For an annotated edition of Iolo's manuscript English translation of his 'Third Series', see further R. Bromwich, *Transactions of the Honourable Society of Cymmrodorion*, 1968 and 1969.]

◆ D. Gwenallt Jones (gol.), **Yr Areithiau Pros** (1934). A selection of the 'Prose Orations', which are here described as exercises in declamation composed for the use of apprentice bards. They consist of short anecdotes, lists of things liked and disliked, imaginary dreams and speeches. They have come down in numerous manuscript copies, none of which is earlier than the sixteenth century, though their contents suggest that those which contain echoes of the Mabinogi and other medieval tales, have developed out of considerably older materials. They were probably evolved gradually by the bards over a long antecedent period. The two first examples here given have phrases culled from 'Culhwch and Olwen', while 'Araith Iolo Goch' is obviously a parody of that tale. The **Areithiau** have been fathered on the names of earlier poets, especially poets of the fourteenth century – Dafydd ap Gwilym, Iolo Goch, Gruffudd ab Adda, Llywelyn Goch ap Meurig Hen.

Medieval Adaptations from Latin and French

Henry Lewis (gol.), **Brut Dingestow** (1942, 1975). An edition of the Dingestow Court version of Brut y Brenhinedd (NLW MS 5266B, 'The History of the Kings'). This is one of three early independent Welsh translations of Geoffrey of Monmouth's *Historia Regum Britanniae*, written during the thirteenth century. According to the ninth-century *Historia Brittonum*, Brutus, or Britto (a fictitious (great) grandson of the Trojan Aeneas), was the first colonizer to come to the Island of Britain. He was regarded as the eponymous ancestor of the Britons and the Welsh, and later was claimed as the direct ancestor of the ruling dynasty of Gwynedd. By extension 'Brut' came to mean 'chronicle, history'. [See further B.F. Roberts, *Brut y Brenhinedd* (Dublin Institute for Advanced Studies, 1971), and idem, 'Geoffrey of Monmouth and Brut y Brenhinedd', chapter iv of **The Arthur of the Welsh** (p.30 below).]

◆ D. Simon Evans, **Historia Gruffud vab Kenan. Gyda Rhagymadrodd a Nodiadau** (1977). An extensive study and edition of the only medieval Welsh biography of a layman: Gruffudd ap Cynan ruled Gwynedd from the late eleventh century until his death in 1137. The **Historia** is a translation, made in the second half of the thirteenth century, from a lost Latin original. In the 300 pages of introduction the editor investigates all historical sources relevant to Gruffudd's life and times, which come from Ireland, Wales and Britain as a whole: the Welsh, Irish, Norse and Anglo-Norman chronicles, annals and records are all examined, together with the relevant Welsh bardic poetry. Linguistic and historical features of the brief text are then fully discussed and annotated, and it is concluded that the original Latin work was composed during the reign of Gruffudd's son, Owain Gwynedd, in order to establish the prestige and authority of his dynasty. [An English translation of the **Historia** by D.S. Evans was published by Llanerch Enterprises in 1990.]

◆ Ifor Williams, **Chwedlau Odo** (The Tales of Odo) (1926, 1957). A selection, from an early thirteenth-century translation of Latin animal fables, by an English cleric named Odo of Cyrinton (Cheriton in Kent). Such parables, in which human characteristics are assigned to animals, are ultimately based on Aesop's fables, and variants of Aesop enjoyed wide popularity all over Europe, not least as *exempla* for use in sermon literature. The text is from Llanstephan 4 (end of fourteenth century). Edited with a comprehensive introduction and notes, which are of much general interest, though intended primarily for young students.

◆ Henry Lewis (gol.), **Chwedleu Seith Doethon Rufein** (1925; new edn 1958, 1967). An edition, with introduction and notes, of fifteen tales from the Welsh adaptation in the Red Book of Hergest of the *Historia Septem Sapientum Romae*. This is a frame-collection of *fabliaux* which circulated widely over Europe from the twelfth century, and which is ultimately of ancient oriental origin. The fourteenth-century Welsh text is a free rendering, rather than a translation, of the Latin original; it contains two tales which are not found in any other version. It recalls the narrative style and traditional openings of the Welsh 'chwedlau', with examples of 'araith' (oration, rhetoric), and phrases which echo the actual wording of passages in 'Culhwch ac Olwen', 'Breuddwyd Maxen' and 'Owein' (texts which are also found in the Red Book). **Chwedleu Seith Doethon Rufein** is the ultimate source for the fable of the faithful hound Gelert, which later became associated with Beddgelert in Snowdonia.

◆ Thomas Jones (gol.), **Y Bibyl Ynghymraec** (1940). A Middle Welsh translation of a part of the Latin *Promptuarium Bibliae* – a summary of mainly Old Testament names, genealogies and events. The text is from Peniarth 20 (most recently dated by Daniel Huws to *c*.1330). An addition links the story with 'Brut y Brenhinedd' and 'Dares Phrygius' by tracing the descent of Eneas

Ysgwydwyn (the progenitor of Brutus) from Japhet, son of Noah. The beginning of the text is defective, and a translation of the first chapter of Genesis has been added from a sixteenth-century copy (believed to come from Peniarth 20) in the hand of Thomas Wiliems, Trefriw. (For excerpts see **Drych yr Oesoedd Canol**, below.)

◆ Nesta Lloyd and Morfydd E. Owen (goln), **Drych yr Oesoedd Canol** (A Mirror of the Middle Ages) (1986). This work enriches the cultural background to the poetry and 'cyfarwyddyd' of the Middle Ages by offering a selection of edited passages from prose works written between the thirteenth and the fifteenth centuries. These are subdivided under the headings of religion, history, law, geography, agriculture, hunting, medicine, etc. The extracts are for the most part medieval translations from Latin (since Latin was then the universal language for the communication and transmission of knowledge). Indigenous Welsh learning is, however, represented by extracts from Cyfraith Hywel (the Law of Hywel), the Triads and the Lives of the Saints, while some archaic concepts of British geography are quoted from the tract on 'The Names of the Island of Britain'. Each section is prefixed by an introductory note, and there is an informative general introduction and a glossary.

◆ D. Simon Evans (ed.), **The Welsh Life of St David** (1988). An early fourteenth-century translation of the Latin Life of the saint by the eleventh-century Rhigyfarch of Llanbadarn Fawr, edited with introduction and notes from the text in the Llyfr Ancr Llanddewibrefi (Jesus Coll. MS 2=119). The extensive introduction discusses the evidence for the cult of St David, with a full account of Rhigyfarch, his family and his literary, cultural and political ambience, the effects of the Norman Conquest on the Church in Wales, and all other questions which are common to the Latin and Welsh Lives of the saint. The unknown Welsh translator may have been a monk attached to St David's or to some other church in the diocese. [This edition partly supersedes DSE's earlier **Buched Dewi** (1959, 1994), which was based on the collation of the text of the Life in Llanstephan 27, with variants cited from other manuscripts. This appeared before J.W. James's definitive edition of **Rhigyfarch's Life of Saint David** became available in 1967 (for which see p.38 below).]

(The four following works all illustrate the high standard in the art of translation and paraphrase from French texts which was attained under the increasing French influences which were brought to bear on Wales during the thirteenth and fourteenth centuries. At the same time, they show how the developing art of translation became fully integrated into the traditional style of Welsh narrative. The tendency of all these Welsh translators, however, was to shorten or to summarize.)

◆ S.J. Williams (gol.), **Ystorya de Carolo Magno** (1930; 2nd edn 1968). Edited translations from parts of a Latin chronicle and French poems relating to Charlemagne, grouped together in the Red Book of Hergest in such a way as to form a cycle. The framework is provided by the *Turpini Historia*, attributed to a certain Madog ap Selyf, who worked under the patronage of a descendant of the Lord Rhys of Deheubarth between 1265 and 1283. Into this is interpolated a translation of the passage from the 'Chanson de Roland' describing the battle of Roncevaux and the hero's death, and a further passage from the French poem 'Otinel'. With introduction, notes and glossary.

◆ Morgan Watkin, **Ystorya Bown de Hamtwn** (1958). Diplomatic edition of the text preserved in the White Book of Rhydderch (*c.*1350–), with introduction and notes. The text is a thirteenth-century translation of a lost Anglo-Norman *Geste de Boun de Hamtone*. It blends elements from romance, epic, folk-tales and saints' legends: the hero fights with dragons and Saracens, travels widely, and marries a (converted) princess. The story was widely popular all over Europe, and exists in many vernacular versions. The Welsh rendering belongs to the same literary milieu as the Charlemagne tales, and the translator's creative language maintains the same high standard as is found in these, with some lively vernacular dialogue. 'Syr Bwn' was known to later Welsh poets as a paragon of courage and Christian virtues.

◆ Patricia Williams, **Kedymdeithyas Amlyn ac Amic** (The Friendship of Amlyn and Amic) (1982). The Welsh version of this famous story from the Red Book of Hergest is a rather free translation of the twelfth-century *Vita Amici et Amelii carissimorum*, a tale known also from its French counterpart *Li Amitiez de Ami et Amile*. Both represent the 'hagiographic' rather than the 'romantic' version of the story of the two friends, which was widely known over Europe, and is marginally associated with the Charlemagne romances (the pair die as martyrs, fighting for Charles). The simple but elegant prose of the Welsh version frequently recalls the speech-patterns of the Mabinogi. It is difficult to date the tale more precisely than as pre-1400, since the existence of a thirteenth-century Anglo-Norman poem, representing the 'romantic' version, may well underlie the emotional evocation of the names of this pair of perfect friends in elegies by the poets Dafydd ap Gwilym and Iolo Goch.

◆ Thomas Jones (gol.), **Ystoryaeu Seint Greal: Rhan 1: Y Keis** (Stories of the Holy Grail: Part 1: The Quest) (1992). Thomas Jones's posthumous work is introduced by J.E. Caerwyn Williams, with an introduction by Ceridwen Lloyd-Morgan, notes and glossary. The **Keis** is an abbreviated translation of the thirteenth-century *Queste del Saint Graal*, edited from the late fourteenth-century manuscript Peniarth 11, with variants from NLW 3063E, and a full discussion of the manuscripts by Daniel Huws. The scribe of Peniarth 11 was Hywel Fychan, who is better known as the main scribe of the Red Book of Hergest. In Peniarth 11 a translation of the romance of Perlesvaus follows as Part 2 of the Grail stories, and an edition of this second part is in preparation.

Discussions

◆ Proinsias Mac Cana, **The Mabinogi** ('Writers of Wales', 1977; new edn 1992). An essential introduction to present-day study of the eleven tales commonly entitled 'The Mabinogion' (an ancient misnomer, whose currency derives from its original adoption in 1849 by Lady Charlotte Guest as the title for her pioneer publication of the tales, with accompanying translation). The authentic title 'Mabinogi' occurs in the manuscripts only in relation to the four mythological tales (=**Pedeir Keinc y Mabinogi**, p.18 above) which are derived from traditions of the ancient Celtic deities – the children of Don and of Llŷr. The Four Branches receive priority as the subject of the first half of Mac Cana's study. His book offers a concise exposition of the leading questions concerning the genesis and significance of all the eleven tales – the Four Branches of the Mabinogi, 'Culhwch and Olwen', the 'Dream of Maxen', 'Lludd and Llefelys', and the Three Romances of 'Owein', 'Gereint' and 'Peredur'. Illuminating parallels with early Irish literature are pointed out at all stages: in particular, the parallel is noted between aspects of the Arthurian cycle and the cycle of Fionn mac Cumhaill.

◆ Proinsias Mac Cana, **Branwen Daughter of Llŷr: A Study of the Irish Affinities and of the Composition of the Second Branch of the Mabinogi** (1958). This early study by the author is significant as representing a distinguished Irish scholar's overview of the Irish analogues, or possible analogues, to incidents in the tale of 'Branwen'. Mac Cana's findings remain valuable, although a later generation would probably be less ready to accept that such analogues are due to direct literary borrowings into Welsh from Irish, rather than the result of a common Celtic inheritance, in which both nations once participated. Certain points of detail in the discussion of 'Branwen' require modification in the light of findings made over the last forty years – for instance in relation to the significance of the Triads quoted, or implied, in the background to the tale, and the variants of specific incidents in the 'Mabinogi' which appear in these and elsewhere. Mac Cana advances an intriguing speculation as to the possible authorship of the Four Branches, and makes perceptive remarks on the author's style.

◆ W.J. Gruffydd, **Math vab Mathonwy** (1928); idem, **Rhiannon** (1953). As early milestones in the study of the Four Branches of the Mabinogi, these two books cannot be disregarded. However much opinions may by now have altered with regard to certain of WJG's findings, they represent an important stage in the evolution of Mabinogi scholarship. A quarter of a century separates the dates of publication of the two books, yet the author's opinion that the 'Mabinogi' developed originally around the life-story of the hero Pryderi, remained virtually unchanged over this long period. (WJG failed to complete his study of 'Branwen', the second Branch; for an outline of his views on this tale see the appendix to Mac Cana's **Branwen** (above), and **Llên Cymru** iv, 129–34.) WJG's approach is that of a folklorist, rather than of a mythologist, yet he followed his teacher Sir John Rhŷs in discerning a number of analogues in early Irish tales, as well as in modern Irish folk-tales, for themes in the 'Mabinogi'. Yet he envisaged these analogues as due to the participation of Wales and Ireland in a common Celtic inheritance, rather than as the result of direct borrowing, whether oral or literary, by the one from the other. He believed that the sources of the constituent stories had been handed down over the centuries since their early evolution in west Wales, in Gwynedd and Dyfed – two areas in which Irish settlements had been made in the remotest past. He believed that originally the tales might even have been first narrated in the Irish language. Yet it remained for a gifted south Wales author, in the eleventh or early twelfth century, to redact the Four Branches in the classic form in which the 'Mabinogi' has come down to us. In the course of his discussion WJG makes a number of valuable identifications of incidents which are introduced in the tales to explain forgotten place-names.

◆ K.H. Jackson, **The International Popular Tale and Early Welsh Tradition** (1961). Professor Jackson brings a new dimension to the study of both the analogues to, and the possible influences upon the 'Mabinogi' and the other Welsh tales. He illustrates by examples the great antiquity and widespread distribution of international story-themes ('folk-tales'), which are attested in countries dispersed throughout the world. He shows that such stories were cultivated in early times by both rich and poor alike, and were in no sense restricted to the peasantry. International themes (such as the 'Calumniated Wife'), which are prominent in the 'Mabinogi', could have reached Britain during the Roman period or at an even earlier date. Both Celtic and international story-themes, though more fully exemplified in early Irish sources than in Welsh, are nevertheless as likely to have reached Britain directly from the Continent as they are to have come from Ireland. KHJ's concluding views on the genesis and authorship of the 'Mabinogi' will be found more controversial.

◆ Pennar Davies, **Rhwng Chwedl a Chredo: Datblygiad Meddwl Crefyddol Cymru yn yr Oesoedd Cynnar** (Between Fable and Belief: the early development of religious thought in Wales) (1966). This book is an expansion of a lecture sponsored by the Pantyfedwen Trust and delivered in 1963. The author demonstrates from early Welsh literature the continuity in thought and ethics which spans the divide between pre-Christian and Christian beliefs: he thus examines the 'Mabinogi' from a viewpoint distinctive from that of any previous writer. The importance of this study lies in its later chapters, which assess the Four Branches of the Mabinogi as a finished literary masterpiece, instead of concentrating on the constituent elements which went in to their formation. The early chapters have been subject to some criticism, as oversimplifying the details of the archaeological background to early Celtic Christianity.

◆ Oliver Davies, **Celtic Christianity in Early Medieval Wales: the Origins of the Welsh Spiritual Tradition** (1996). This book uncovers the origins of a Welsh spiritual tradition in the early religious literature which OD sees as reflecting the interaction of early Christianity with pagan Celtic religion. OD approaches his subject from a wide European perspective and intersperses his commentary and interpretation with extensive English translations of his own from sources such as the Black Book of Carmarthen, the Book of Taliesin and the Lives of the Saints.

◆ Ifor Williams, **Chwedl Taliesin** (1957). Based on the O'Donnell lecture delivered in the University of Wales for the year 1955–6. The 'Story of Taliesin' is shown to be of ancient pagan and mythological origin, although in its complete form it has come down only in versions recorded from the sixteenth century and later. (A translation of one of these is given in Guest's *Mabinogion*; see also P.K. Ford, **Ystoria Taliesin** p.20 above.) IW outlines the earliest of these versions, as it has come down in the text of Elis Gruffydd (the 'soldier of Calais', *c.*1490–1552), adding to it some interesting notes on names and places. His belief was that a semi-mythological story about Taliesin was first evolved in north Wales during the ninth or tenth century, and he finds confirmation for this in early poems preserved in the fourteenth-century Book of Taliesin: these clearly have their context in events narrated in the story. Evidently, 'Chwedl Taliesin' enjoyed a wide circulation in Wales over a period of several centuries: a number of new poems were added in the later versions, and these show how the tale became progressively christianized at the hands of its later transmitters.

◆ Sioned Davies, **Crefft y Cyfarwydd** (The Art of the 'Cyfarwydd') (1996). The eleven tales in the 'Mabinogion' collection are envisaged as literary compositions deriving their essential features from the techniques of the 'Cyfarwydd' or oral storyteller: episodic structure, recurrent formulaic elements, triple repetitions and conversations in direct speech. The stories were intended to be declaimed or read aloud to a listening audience. Comparisons are made with oral literatures elsewhere, and current theories about oral composition are discussed.

Arthurian Studies

◆ Rachel Bromwich, A.O.H. Jarman and Brynley F. Roberts (eds.), **The Arthur of the Welsh** (1991, 1992, 1993; pb. 1995). This book contains thirteen studies by scholars from universities in Wales and England, and from the National Library of Wales, which offer a comprehensive survey of medieval Arthurian literature, as composed either in the Welsh language, or in Latin by men with Welsh connections. The first chapters investigate problems surrounding the alleged 'historical' Arthur, and the earliest traditions as revealed in chronicles and poetry; subsequent chapters discuss in turn Geoffrey of Monmouth; the Merlin Legend; the Triads and the Lives of the Saints; the altering and developing presentation of Arthur in 'Culhwch and Olwen' and in the different 'Mabinogion' tales; Arthur in Brittany; the evidence relating to Tintagel and other famous 'Arthurian' sites in south-west Britain; the transference into Anglo-Norman and French of some Celtic personal names (including 'Drystan' > 'Tristan') and story-themes from early Welsh and Breton traditional tales; and the later reassimilation of continental Arthurian material into Welsh. An introduction by the editors gives a broad outline of some of the fundamental problems, and includes a palaeographer-librarian's authoritative account (by Daniel Huws) of the most important early Welsh manuscripts which contain the Arthurian poems, triads and stories. A companion volume **The Arthur of the English** is in preparation and expected to be published in 1999, with **The Arthur of the Germans** to follow.

◆ A.O.H. Jarman, **The Legend of Merlin** (1960, 1970). Professor Jarman's inaugural lecture gives a clear and succinct outline of views which he later developed more fully in a number of articles, in Welsh and in English (the most recent one is in **The Arthur of the Welsh**), concerning the pre-history of the legendary Merlin, as this figure is presented by Geoffrey of Monmouth and in the continental romances. Geoffrey's Merlin derives from a combination of traditions preserved in Welsh poetry concerning the poet-prophet Myrddin (see Jarman's **Ymddiddan Myrddin a Thaliesin** p.6 above), and the unrelated tale of the wonder-child Ambrosius, which he derived from the *Historia Brittonum*. An extended knowledge of Celtic traditions, acquired at a later date, is reflected in Geoffrey of Monmouth's poem the 'Vita Merlini'.

◆ Basil Clarke (ed.), **Life of Merlin: Geoffrey of Monmouth's Vita Merlini** (1973). Edited with facing translation, introduction, textual commentary, name-notes and bibliography, together with appendices which give quotations from relevant Celtic source-material. The 'Vita Merlini' is a poem in 1,529 Latin hexameters, which is believed to have been composed by Geoffrey of Monmouth about 1150 – some fifteen years after the appearance of that writer's *Historia Regum Britanniae*, and reflecting the increased knowledge of Welsh poems and Triads and other Celtic tradition which Geoffrey had evidently acquired during the intervening years. The complete text of the poem exists only in a single manuscript of the late thirteenth century (Cotton Vespasian E iv), though a number of manuscript fragments have also survived. The 'Vita Merlini' was last edited by E. Faral (Paris, 1929), following on the publication of J.J. Parry's American edition of 1925: both are now difficult to obtain, and have been superseded by more recent work on the Celtic background material. Considerable advances have been made in the understanding of the Welsh and Irish cognates and sources of the poem: all of these are reflected in the apparatus to BC's careful edition. The 'Vita Merlini' has a special importance as supplementing from lost sources the Welsh traditions about Myrddin Wyllt: it also presents an essential facet to the portrayal of Merlin in Arthurian romance.

◆ Glenys Goetinck, **Peredur: A Study of Welsh Tradition in the Grail Legends** (1975). A useful survey, which draws on contemporary scholarship to examine the Welsh and Irish tales which are relevant to the Celtic background of the Grail romances. There is a general discussion of the theme of 'sovereignty', which she discerns in each of the Three Romances

– 'Owein', 'Gereint' and 'Peredur' – and this is followed by a more detailed study of the tale of 'Peredur'. (Later opinion, however, as reflected in **The Arthur of the Welsh** and elsewhere, records a lack of general agreement with the writer's belief in the individual, rather than separate authorship, of the Three Romances.) An appendix examines the complex relationship subsisting between the four existing manuscript copies of 'Peredur'. (See also G. Goetinck's edition of **Historia Peredur vab Efrawc**, p.26 above.)

♦ Constance Bullock-Davies, **Professional Interpreters and the Matter of Britain** (1966). This essay broke new ground on the subject of the cultural and linguistic interchanges which took place between the Welsh and the Anglo-Normans, both before and after the Norman Conquest, and CBD's study has especial relevance for the transmission of Celtic names and stories into Arthurian Romance. She emphasizes the importance of the highly-qualified *latimarii* or professional interpreters, attached to the courts of kings and princes, who acted both as translators and also as messengers and negotiators. Drawing on original research into pedigrees, Latin charters, and the Pipe Roll, she has identified among these the famous Bledericus or Bledri *latimer* (who worked for King Henry I), and Iorwerth Goch of Powys 'king's *latimer* in Wales' who is familiar, though in a different capacity, from the 'Dream of Rhonabwy'. Did the activities of these men include the transmission of Welsh 'cyfarwyddiadau' to the Norman families with whom they lived and worked? No certainty on this point is possible, but CBD emphasizes that a basic distinction must be drawn between the original translators, and the less well-endowed entertainers who subsequently transmitted the Welsh tales to the Normans.

Language, Grammar and Dictionaries

◆ Janet Davies, **The Welsh Language** (1993). A summary introduction to all aspects of the Welsh language, and from every angle – linguistic, literary, historical and sociological; the institutions, traditions, and every kind of modern social and cultural development. Welsh – by far the oldest language spoken in Britain – shares features with other languages of the Indo-European language family, and within this family has closer relationships with Irish and Gaelic, and with its even closer siblings Breton and Cornish, as fellow-members of the Celtic language group. The history, development and principal linguistic features of the Welsh language are all clearly set forth. Most distinctive of the linguistic features are the initial (and originally medial) consonantal mutations, which are common to all the Celtic tongues. Despite minor dialect variations in the spoken language between north and south Wales, the evolution of a single literary language was nurtured from an early date – through the different texts of the 'Law of Hywel', the 'Mabinogi', the indigenous tales, and adaptations from all kinds of foreign literary works and prose treatises on a variety of subjects. This unified development culminated in William Morgan's Bible of 1588, 'an exalted model of correct and majestic Welsh', which drew on all the previous resources of the language. Within such a comprehensive survey of all things Welsh as is here provided, it is hardly possible that more than very brief attention could be paid to the writings of the early and medieval period. But some essentials are given: a page is devoted to the Cynfeirdd, with a facsimile from the manuscript of the 'Gododdin', preceded by a reproduction of the poignant memorial to a family of four on the eighth(?)-century inscribed stone at Tywyn, Meirionydd – *tricet nitanam* (elsewhere interpreted by Ifor Williams as 'grief and loss remain', see **The Beginnings of Welsh Poetry** (p.5).). The many maps, plates and reproductions of pages from early printed books, the inset quotations exemplifying categories of borrowed words, together with excerpts from famous poems, are further attractive features of the book. Bibliographical references are unfortunately minimal.

◆ Henry Lewis, **Datblygiad yr Iaith Gymraeg** (1931; revised edn 1946, 1994). This concise outline of the development of the Welsh language to the end of the medieval period was welcomed on its first appearance as an original work of synthesis, and it has remained the standard treatment of the subject for over sixty years. Three stages in the evolution of the language are identified: i) Early Welsh (elsewhere termed more appropriately 'Primitive Welsh') to the end of the eighth century. During nearly four centuries of the Roman occupation of Britain, when Latin was the dominant language, the fully inflected speech of the Britons lost its inflected endings. This stage is exemplified only by names preserved on inscriptions, in a few Latin writings, and in some later copies; ii) Old Welsh, from the ninth to the eleventh centuries, represented by glosses on Latin works and by a few pieces of consecutive prose; iii) Medieval Welsh, from the twelfth to the fourteenth centuries, exemplified by the competent technical prose of the Law codes, the literary artistry of the 'Mabinogi', and the rich diversity of the variant *genres* exhibited in poetry. From these beginnings there evolved the poetic language of the succeeding 'cywydd' period, and this provided a secure literary base for the diction of Bishop Morgan's Bible of 1588, a work which set a lasting standard for literary Welsh prose. The book includes a chapter on syntax (which indicates how the dialects retained certain archaic forms which became obsolete in literary Welsh) and some account of loan-words. For these, see also H. Lewis, **Yr Elfen Ladin yn yr Iaith Gymraeg** (1943, 1980).

◆ T.J. Morgan, **Y Treigladau a'u Cystrawen** (The Mutations and their Syntax) (1952, 1989). An unprecedented attempt, in nearly five hundred pages, to demonstrate hard and fast grammatical rules as governing the syntax of the initial consonantal mutations, both in the spoken language and in written Welsh of all periods. Although it has been shown that no such comprehensive rules are warranted by the facts, TJM's overall survey constitutes an indispensable work of reference, and an essential point of departure for any future studies of the subject. There are inevitably gaps in the literary sources which have been consulted, and little distinction has been made between dialectal differences in the spoken language; nor is there any reference to the corresponding mutations in the other Celtic languages, or to the instances in 'canu caeth' in which the mutations have been manipulated to suit the demands of 'cynghanedd'. (These points were made in a review by J.E. Caerwyn Williams, **Llên Cymru** ii (1953) which is an essential commentary on the contents of the book.)

◆ D.S. Evans, **Gramadeg Cymraeg Canol** (1951; pb. 1995). A descriptive grammar of medieval Welsh, as found in prose and verse texts recorded in writing between the twelfth and fourteenth centuries. Illustrative quotations are given from the Cynfeirdd and the Gogynfeirdd, the 'Mabinogi' and a wide range of prose texts, including medieval translations into Welsh. The historical development of the language is indicated by the frequent notes which look back to earlier word-forms attested in Old Welsh sources. [DSE's English counterpart to **Gramadeg Cymraeg Canol**, *A Grammar of Middle Welsh* (Dublin Institute for Advanced Studies 1964, 1989) is not a close translation of the Welsh edition, since almost all sections in the earlier book have been considerably extended. A new and valuable introduction surveys all published sources for Old and Middle Welsh verse and prose, and translations are given for all examples cited from early sources to illustrate points of grammar. But **Gramadeg Cymraeg Canol** will remain an essential work of reference for all concerned with the study of the language in any depth, since it familiarizes the student with the appropriate Welsh linguistic and grammatical terms.]

◆ Stephen J. Williams, **Elfennau Gramadeg Cymraeg** (1959; revised edn 1980; pb. 1990); idem, **A Welsh Grammar** (1980, 1993). This grammar of standard literary Welsh follows closely the arrangement of J. Morris-Jones's *Elementary Welsh Grammar* (Oxford, 1921) and idem, *A Welsh Grammar* (Oxford, 1913, 1925). But it takes account of more recent contributions to the study of accidence and syntax, which have been published by scholars in the **Bulletin of the Board of Celtic Studies** and elsewhere; the author acknowledges a particular debt to the works of Henry Lewis. Illustrative examples are drawn principally from William Morgan's Bible of 1588. The English **Grammar** is a close translation of the Welsh version, with occasional added notes, and some minor rearrangements. English translations are given for most of the examples quoted from original sources.

◆ J. Lloyd-Jones, **Geirfa Barddoniaeth Gynnar Gymraeg** (Glossary of Early Welsh Poetry). Originally published in eight parts: vol. 1 *A–Enrydedd* (1931–46); vol. 2 *Enryuedd–Heilic* (1950–63). This work was compiled in response to an early request from the Board of Celtic Studies for a dictionary of the poetry of the Gogynfeirdd. It draws principally on J.G. Evans's diplomatic editions of the early poetry (pp.1–2 above), but these are supplemented by additional references to a wide range of published texts. The **Geirfa** represents the life's work of a single devoted scholar: it merits the title of 'Geiriadur' or 'Dictionary', rather than the lesser one of a mere 'Geirfa' or 'Vocabulary'. Most unfortunately it was left unfinished at its author's death.

◆ **Geiriadur Prifysgol Cymru: A Dictionary of the Welsh Language** (1950–). The compilation of a historical dictionary of Welsh on the lines of the *Oxford English Dictionary* was planned by the Board of Celtic Studies in 1920, soon after the Board's foundation. Almost thirty years were spent in the preliminary collection of material on slips, before the work was sufficiently advanced for the first fascicule to be published in 1950, under the initial editorship of R.J. Thomas, with Ifor Williams as consultant editor. Equivalents for words are given in both Welsh and English. Illustrative examples are quoted from both the written and the spoken language, and from sources which demonstrate the variant and changing significance of words, from their earliest to their latest occurrences. Both manuscripts and printed texts are drawn upon up to *c.*1800, and are followed by selected examples indicative of the intensive growth of the Welsh language during the last and the present century, including new additions drawn from the vocabulary of the arts and sciences, the media and administration. Material prepared by J. Lloyd Jones, but left unpublished in his **Geirfa** at the time of his death, has been incorporated in the entries following the letter *h-*. Under the current editorship of Gareth A. Bevan and his team of assistants, it is envisaged that the third of the three large volumes comprising **Geiriadur Prifysgol Cymru** will be completed before the end of the century.

Background

♦ P.C. Bartrum, **Early Welsh Genealogical Tracts** (1966). Genealogical lore was passed down by word of mouth, and from time immemorial, as an essential part of the bardic heritage. Gerald of Wales records that in addition to their remarkable stores of memory, the bards preserved the genealogies of their princes 'in their ancient and authentic books . . . which were written in Welsh'. In this work PCB has assembled, for the first and only time in book form, the early genealogies which are essential for the documentation of medieval Welsh history and tradition. The genealogical tracts which PCB has here edited, indexed, annotated and cross-referenced were nearly all originally composed before the end of the thirteenth century. Some of the later texts and variants have never been published before. The latest persons to be listed are Llywelyn the Great and a few of his contemporaries: one genealogy alone terminates with Llywelyn's grandson, Llywelyn the Last Prince. These genealogies are hardly the less interesting and important for the fact that at almost any stage they may have been contaminated by ulterior motives on the part of their transmitters, or by later scribal carelessness, or because they undoubtedly contain a proportion of legendary and fictitious names. Bartrum's collection opens with the extended inscription on the Valle Crucis pillar, which traces the descent of the ninth-century rulers of Powys to the remote past, with the names of Maximus and Vortigern. An edition of this inscription is followed by the genealogies from the *Historia Brittonum*, from the important Harleian and Jesus College manuscripts, the 'Brychan' documents, the 'Bonedd y Saint' and genealogies from the *Vitae* of the Welsh saints, the Chronicle of the Princes, and other important associated texts. There has as yet been no reissue of this important volume, essential as it is for all medieval Welsh literary and historical studies. [Some corrections to **Early Welsh**

Genealogical Tracts, and a few misprints, have been noted by Bartrum in the **Bulletin of the Board of Celtic Studies** xx (1993), 171–2. P.C. Bartrum's **Welsh Genealogies 300–1400** (1974), in eight volumes, and *Welsh Genealogies 1400–1500* (National Library of Wales, 1983) are both available in microfiche.]

◆ A.W. Wade-Evans (ed.), **Vitae Sanctorum Britanniae et Genealogiae** (1944). The Lives of the Welsh Saints from Cotton Vespasian A14, written by various hands *c*.1200 (probably at Brecon or Monmouth Priory); Latin text with facing English translation. The oldest *Vitae* are those of St David by Rhigyfarch (see next entry) and of St Cadog by Lifris of Llancarfan, both attributed to the late eleventh century. The Lives of Illtud, Padarn, Cybi, Carannog and others are of the twelfth century. Also included here are the Welsh Life of St Beuno (untranslated) from *Llyfr Ancr Llanddewi Brefi* (ed. J. Morris-Jones, Oxford, 1894), the 'Brychan' documents, and a fourteenth-century text of 'Bonedd y Saint' (for the last two see entries in **Early Welsh Genealogical Tracts** above). This book has been criticized on the ground of inadequate editing, and a new edition is much needed. Nevertheless, it has never been superseded (except in respect of the Life of St David, see next entry). It is the only available edition of these important *Vitae Sanctorum*, since that of W.J. Rees, *Lives of the Cambro-British Saints* (Llandovery, 1853).

◆ J.W. James (ed.), **Rhigyfarch's Life of St. David** (1967, 1985). This is the definitive edition of the *Vita Davidis* by Rhigyfarch of Llanbadarn (1056/7–99), son of Sulien, who was twice bishop of St David's. The text is based on a full collation of twenty-nine manuscripts, many of which had not previously been brought to light. Among these Dr James distinguishes five recensions, and selects those of 'Nero' and 'Digby' (both of the mid-twelfth century) as coming closest to Rhigyfarch's original work, which is believed to have been composed *c*.1090. He adopts BL Nero Ei as his basic text, and notes all significant variants from this. It is suggested that this recension shows the influence of the twelfth-century attempts by Bishop Bernard of St David's to win archiepiscopal status for his see, together with Welsh ecclesiastical independence from Canterbury. The introduction relates entirely to the formation of the text and its recensions, and is not concerned with the content of the Life. An English translation follows the Latin text. [For the **Welsh Life of St David**, see p.24 above.]

◆ F.G. Bowen, **Saints, Scaways, and Settlements** (1969; new edn 1977, 1988). A geographical survey of the spheres of influence reflected by the cults of fifth- and sixth-century saints in Wales, Cornwall and Brittany, EGB emphasizes the unifying force held by the western sea-routes between these countries, centred on the Irish sea. Dedications to a particular saint do not imply the foundation of a church by him or by one of his followers: rather, they are indications of that saint's sphere of influence, and they frequently represent much older traditions than those which are preserved in the *Vitae*. The extent of the later dioceses, often established by the Normans, tend to reflect ancient and even prehistoric cultural areas, whose integrity had survived intact into the Age of the Saints (fifth to seventh centuries). A geographical survey of the cults of particular saints – Dewi, Cadog, Illtud, Beuno, the Brychan family – is extended to include Kentigern of Glasgow (renamed Cyndeyrn Garthwys in the Welsh 'Bonedd y Saint') whose cult extended over Cumbria and into north Wales. (This book is an enlarged replacement of the author's **The Settlements of the Celtic Saints in Wales**, 1954.)

◆ G.H. Doble, **Lives of the Welsh Saints**. Edited with an introduction by D. Simon Evans (1971, 1983). Canon Doble (1880–1945) is principally known for his life-long studies – published locally in a series of booklets – of nearly fifty Cornish saints, several of whom were also remembered in Wales. Late in his life Doble turned his attention to a closer study of the sixth-century founders of the Welsh Church. In 1940–4 he published his 'Welsh Saints' series of booklets, which were described by a reviewer as 'in the best traditions of modern scholarship'. These contained his accounts of the Latin *Vitae* of five Welsh saints – Dubricius (Dyfrig), Teilo, Oudoceus (Euddogwy), Illtud and Paulinus, based on the Lives in the Book of Llandâf, except for that of the Breton saint Paulinus (who came traditionally from Glamorgan) which is by the Breton monk Wrmonoc. All of these saints were near-contemporaries of St David, and belonged, like him, to areas in south and south-west Wales. Doble's studies, which had long been out of print, are here reissued, with the permission of the Dean and Chapter of Truro Cathedral. There are very few editorial alterations, but D. Simon Evans has added to the text some explanatory footnotes, together with a long and informative introduction on 'Our Early Welsh Saints and History'.

◆ Glanmor Williams, **The Welsh Church from Conquest to Reformation** (1962; revised edn 1976). This important study surveys the two-and-a-half eventful and chaotic centuries which followed the Edwardian Conquest of Wales in 1282–3. Literature, society and history are closely intertwined throughout the discussion, and GW makes ample cross-references to the rich literary inheritance of the period, in both prose and in verse, as essential for the correct interpretation of the relatively sparse historical records. Here is to be found the fullest analysis and discussion to date of the collection of religious texts in the Llyfr Ancr Llanddewibrefi (1346), which 'marks the highest point in the development of philosophical and theological literature in medieval Wales'; with accounts of the Welsh biblical apocrypha, and of other religious works first translated into Welsh during these years. There is a perceptive discussion of the two major poets of the period – Dafydd ap Gwilym and Iolo Goch – and of the most significant aspects of their poetry, including their variant reactions to the altered and developing society of post-Conquest Wales. The Church in Wales is envisaged in its wider setting, as a small and remote, but integral member of western Christendom.

◆ R.R. Davies et al. (eds), **Welsh Society and Nationhood: Historical Essays Presented to Glanmor Williams** (1984). The earlier of the nine studies in this book are of especial relevance to medieval Welsh literature. In 'Gildas, Maelgwn and the Bards' J.E. Caerwyn-Williams examines the powerful role of poets in early Celtic society in the context of Gildas's diatribe against Maelgwn Gwynedd, and he cites examples to illustrate the mutual dependence between the poets and the kings and princes whom they both evaluated and served. David Walker's 'Cultural Survival in an Age of Conquest' documents 'the agony of conquest for those who were defeated' in relation to the Norman Conquest and its dissimilar effects in England and in Wales; he presents Gerald of Wales as representative of the post-Conquest generation, ambivalently conscious of having inherited from each of the two traditions. R.R. Davies in 'Law and National Identity in Thirteenth-Century Wales' examines further the clash of cultures, and the significance of 'Cyfraith Hywel' ('customary law' as distinct from 'prince-made law'). This was hardly less of a focus than the possession of a distinctive language and common traditions of origin for the awareness of national identity which was evolving during a century which saw the rise of Gwynedd to be the predominant power in Wales.

◆ T.M. Charles-Edwards, **The Welsh Laws** ('Writers of Wales', 1989). This book gives a succinct account of medieval Welsh law – 'Cyfraith Hywel'. The codification of the Laws goes back to the time of Hywel Dda (Howel the Good) a mid tenth-century ruler of Dyfed, who in his later life held authority over almost the whole of Wales. The Laws are preserved in a number of manuscripts, from the thirteenth to the sixteenth centuries. 'Cyfraith Hywel' was an organic growth, which gradually became accommodated to altering circumstances throughout the Middle Ages and beyond: even after the Act of Union 'Cyfraith Hywel' continued to be partly operative in such matters as inheritance and personal status. The three main versions in which the Laws have come down are known as the Books of Cyfnerth (the earliest), Blegywryd, and Iorwerth respectively. The Latin texts are recognized as among the most important of the law-books, and the earliest of all the texts is one in Latin. But in view of the preponderance of very early Welsh technical terms in 'Cyfraith Hywel', it is impossible to ascertain whether the Laws were originally redacted in Latin or in Welsh. It is recognized that from the earliest times there has been a close relation between the clarity and concise style of the Laws and the development of a lucid prose style for other writings in medieval Welsh: the two went hand-in-hand. This is exemplified most strikingly in the 'Mabinogi' and in the other tales and translations. Saunders Lewis described 'Cyfraith Hywel' as 'a pinnacle of European medieval culture' and as 'the cornerstone of the Welsh language'.

TMCE concludes his brief survey with a useful bibliography which lists the Press's editions of the Latin and Welsh versions of 'Cyfraith Hywel', and the manuscripts (mainly preserved in the National Library of Wales) from which these are drawn: H.D.

Emanuel, **Latin Texts of the Welsh Laws** (1967); S.J. Williams and J. Enoch Powell, **Llyfr Blegywryd** (1942; 2nd edn 1961), A.R. Wiliam, **Llyfr Iorwerth** (1960, 1979); D. Jenkins, **Llyfr Colan** (1963, 1980). He adds a further full list of published studies of the Laws: this includes D. Jenkins and M.E. Owen (eds), **The Welsh Law of Women** (1980) and T.M. Charles-Edwards, M.E. Owen and D.B. Walters (eds), **Lawyers and Laymen** (1986).

[For an English translation of 'Cyfraith Hywel', with introduction and notes, see Dafydd Jenkins, *Hywel Dda; The Law* (Llandysul, 1986). The volume next listed also includes an important essay on the Laws.]

◆ Elwyn Davies (ed.), **Celtic Studies in Wales: A Survey** (1963). Though now over thirty years old, this book retains its value and usefulness as an outline of advances made in Welsh scholarship to 1963, in the several fields within the remit of the University of Wales's Board of Celtic Studies. The book was originally published as an introduction to the subject for the participants at the Second International Congress of Celtic Studies, held in Cardiff in that year. In spite of extensive subsequent developments in the various fields which are covered (including the need for extensions to the bibliography, see pp.43–4 below), each of the five chapters in the book remain useful and valuable: Leslie Alcock, 'Celtic Archaeology and Art'; A.H. Dodd, 'Welsh History and Historians'; H.D. Emanuel, 'Studies in the Welsh Laws'; R. Geraint Gruffydd, 'Literature'; T. Arwyn Watkins, 'Language and Linguistics'. A preface by Henry Lewis gives a brief description of the activities of the Board of Celtic Studies, with a list of the Board's earlier publications.

General Literary Guides

Meic Stephens (gol.), **Cydymaith i Lenyddiaeth Cymru** (1986, 1993); idem (ed.), *A Companion to the Literature of Wales* (Oxford, 1986). This is a Welsh literary encyclopedia and a useful factual guide to much else of contingent interest. The **Cydymaith** and the *Companion* were published simultaneously in Welsh and in English, with the text corresponding between the two versions. The many hundreds of entries are anonymous, and are in each instance by the same writer, whether originally composed in Welsh or in English (or both). Each edition contains close on 700 pages and is the work of 222 individual contributors whose names are listed at the beginning. The core of the work gives an account of famous historical characters and events: of poets, historians, chroniclers, theologians, scholars, etc. (limited in the first edition to people born not later than 1950). In addition to entries on individuals, there are subject entries which list places of famous historical, literary, or legendary interest; cathedrals, abbeys, monasteries and famous mansions; religious denominations; chronicles, societies, institutions; academies, periodicals and journals; famous poems, plays and novels; characters and incidents in legend and mythology; Welsh poetic terms and metres – and much else besides. (New and extended editions are in preparation. Both the Welsh and English editions will be published by the University of Wales Press in 1997 and 1998 respectively.)

◆ Thomas Parry, Merfyn Morgan and Gareth Watts (goln), **Llyfryddiaeth Llenyddiaeth Gymraeg** (Bibliography of Welsh Literature) (1976, 1993). A full bibliography of Welsh language and literature was planned in 1962, under the auspices of the Board of Celtic Studies. It was subsequently found to be impractical to combine language and literature in a single work, owing to the sheer volume of material to be included. The compilation of a bibliography of Welsh literature was therefore undertaken as a preliminary, and the first volume (Parry and Morgan) was followed by a second in 1993, edited by Gareth O. Watts. These two volumes together record all known published works concerning Welsh literature, up to 1975 in the case of the first volume, and with additions for the years 1976–86 in the second. This coverage omits only a few instances in which later studies have superseded an older book or article, except in a few cases in which the work possesses an intrinsic interest in itself, as representing a contemporary response to the subject concerned. The principle of classification corresponds in the two volumes: for the medieval period this is primarily dictated by the subject matter, while for the later period the classification is by centuries. There are concluding sections on the various Welsh literary forms in prose and in verse, with a separate section on the Eisteddfod and related matters. Further bibliographical sections list the works of individual scholars, giving references to obituaries and discussions of their published works. The names of the contributors to the individual sections are given in the first volume, and selected references to important reviews are cited.

◆ J.E. Caerwyn Williams (gol.), **Llyfryddiaeth yr Iaith Gymraeg**: trefnwyd gan Marian Beech Hughes (A Bibliography of the Welsh Language: arranged by MBH) (1988). This bibliography supplements in two ways the volumes noted above. It gives a comprehensive list of published work describing the Indo-European origin of the Celtic languages, with works on their early history, both on the continent of Europe and in Britain and Ireland. This is followed by separate sections on each language, which cite works on their individual histories, distribution, grammar, dialects, orthography, personal and place-names. The languages are discussed in the following order: Gwyddeleg (Irish), Gaeleg yr Alban (Scottish Gaelic), Manaweg (Manx), Brythoneg (Brittonic, that is the relationship between Welsh, Cornish and Breton, together with the 'British Latin' spoken in Roman Britain), then separate sections on Cernyweg (Cornish), Llydaweg (Breton) and Cymraeg (Welsh). The second part of the book supplements the two volumes of the **Llyfryddiaeth** noted above by listing works which were published after 1986 relating to Welsh literature; included also are references to unpublished university theses. The sections relating to 'Y Cyfnod Cynnar' (the early period) include works on the inscriptions, the early glosses and other survivals of Old Welsh, as well as on the Hengerdd (the earliest poetry); 'Y Cyfnod Canol' (the middle period) details work on the Gogynfeirdd or Poets of the Princes (to 1988) as well as on the medieval tales, the Laws, and historical and religious works (there is, however, some intentional overlap here with the two previous volumes).

◆ Thomas Parry, **Hanes Llenyddiaeth Gymraeg hyd 1900** (1945, 1979; reprint of 4th edn 1993). Fifty years since its first publication this history of Welsh literature, by one of the century's leading Welsh scholars, remains the standard work on the subject. But it is likely that this estimate now stands more securely in relation to the earlier literature than to that of more recent centuries. In his foreword Sir Thomas Parry states that he was encouraged to undertake a comprehensive survey of Welsh literature because the 1920s and 1930s had seen the publication of the fundamental studies by John Morris-Jones, Ifor Williams, John Lloyd-Jones, G.J. Williams, and a galaxy of other scholars who are named. Parry surveys perceptively the work of his predecessors on the Hengerdd (the earliest poetry), and on the classics of medieval prose; he discusses the Gogynfeirdd more briefly. A complete chapter is devoted to Dafydd ap Gwilym – the only poet to whom this honour is accorded – and this chapter anticipates views more fully expounded ten years later in Parry's definitive edition of the poet's work, **Gwaith Dafydd ap Gwilym** (p.12 above). A general chapter follows on the Cywyddwyr of the fourteenth and following centuries (the 'cywydd' metre was a major innovation by poets of Dafydd ap Gwilym's generation). Parry describes his purpose as being to trace the essential continuity of the Welsh literary tradition through the centuries, and without reference to the question of foreign influences, impacts, or cognate features which are found elsewhere (except in a few instances in which he cites striking parallels in Irish). In the absence of footnote references, the **Hanes Llenyddiaeth** concludes with a twelve-page bibliography, which relates in turn to the subject matter of the successive chapters. (Minor additions and corrections were made to this bibliography in the 1953 edition, but the bibliography was discarded in its entirety from the edition of 1979 and from subsequent reprints, allegedly because of the publication in the interval of Parry's **Llyfryddiaeth Llenyddiaeth Gymraeg** in 1978. This has been a most unfortunate omission, in view of the perennial need of students for a selective bibliography. [For an English translation of Parry's **Hanes Llenyddiaeth Gymraeg** see H.I. Bell, *A History of Welsh Literature*, Oxford, 1955.]

◆ Dafydd Johnston, **A Pocket Guide to the Literature of Wales** (1994). Despite its concise format (137pp) this attractively produced booklet gives a comprehensive survey of Welsh literature down to the present day, and from its earliest recorded beginnings in the sixth century. It forms an excellent supplement which updates Thomas Parry's **Hanes Llenyddiaeth Gymraeg** (see above). It is also fair to say that a fundamental review of earlier scholarship has rarely been accomplished in so creative and yet appreciative a manner, and with so striking a display of original insights on points of detail. DJ takes due account of the changing views and new perspectives which have appeared with the advances in scholarship made over the last fifty years; some of these have been brought to bear upon the interpretations of the earliest poetry advanced in the pre-war years by Ifor Williams, and reflected in Parry's book. Recent developments have included some innovative studies and some greatly improved editions (now in continued progress) of medieval poetry. In this book for the first time literature in the Welsh language is associated with English literature inspired by a Welsh background, and the claim made by its title is implicitly restated – that the literature of Wales in either of its two languages is to be regarded as a single unit originating from an integrated tradition. Yet the first two thirds of the book are concerned exclusively with works composed and transmitted in the Welsh language alone; and apart from a few incidental forecasts in the earlier centuries 'Anglo-Welsh' literature made its earliest substantial appearance in the 1930s. Inset on the pages of the book are the author's own accurate prose translations of Welsh verse (a few translations by others have also been included); there are pages with reproductions from famous manuscripts, and in conclusion a brief bibliography which concentrates on scholarly works published during the last two decades. Attention may also be drawn here to the two companion 'Pocket Guides': J. Graham

Jones, **The History of Wales** (1990, 1995); and Trefor M. Owen, **The Customs and Traditions of Wales** (1991, 1995).

♦ R. Geraint Gruffydd (gol.), **Meistri'r Canrifoedd: Ysgrifau ar Hanes Llenyddiaeth Gymraeg gan Saunders Lewis** (1973, 1982) (Masters of the Centuries: Essays on the History of Welsh Literature). Thirty-seven essays, lectures and reviews by the late Saunders Lewis are here collected from a wide range of periodicals, in which they were originally published over a number of years. The essays include much of Saunders Lewis's most mature literary criticism and discussion, including nearly all that he wrote which is relevant to the medieval period. Among these are his original, if controversial, articles on the genesis of the Four Branches of the Mabinogi, one of his two review articles on Parry's **Gwaith Dafydd ap Gwilym** (p.12 above), essays on the earliest of the Cywyddwyr and on individuals among their successors, including Dafydd Nanmor and Tudur Aled. Included also is his famous Eisteddfod lecture of 1965 on the poet Ann Griffiths. RGG comments on the vision and perception displayed in these essays, and observes that they are valuable not only as literary commentary and analysis, but are distinguished as literature in their own right. Welsh literature is here presented by Saunders Lewis as a small but unique contribution to the literature of Christian Europe.

♦ Alun R. Jones and Gwyn Thomas (eds), **Presenting Saunders Lewis** (1973, 1991). The authors point out that Saunders Lewis has done more than almost any other single writer to introduce the life and culture of Wales to an extended English-reading audience. This book supplements **Meistri'r Canrifoedd** by giving the text of the majority of his lectures, speeches and writings which were originally composed or delivered in English. These lectures and addresses arose mainly from the events of SL's political career, in the course of which, among his other concerns, he laid emphasis on Welsh literature as Wales's most essential spiritual inheritance. The book contains three seminal literary articles: 'The Tradition of Taliesin' develops views earlier anticipated in his **Braslun** (p.16 above), by envisaging Taliesin's praises of Urien Rheged in the sixth century as having established a model for praise-poetry which was reiterated in various ways over many centuries. Included also is his English review article on Parry's **Dafydd ap Gwilym** (reproduced from *Blackfriars* xxxiv (1953), which is to be distinguished by its different range of reference from the separate Welsh review reproduced in **Meistri'r Canrifoedd**). There is a short but significant essay on 'The Essence of Welsh Literature': this cites SL's discovery of a little-known poem by an eighteenth-century 'bardd gwlad' (country poet) from west Wales, in celebration of the launching of a ship, which is a powerful demonstration of the long continuity of the poetic tradition. The book concludes with translations by Gwyn Thomas and Emyr Humphreys of a selection of SL's poems and plays. **Presenting Saunders Lewis** complements **Meistri'r Canrifoedd** in bringing together a very full conspectus of Saunders Lewis's unique contribution to Welsh literature, life and thought.

♦ J.E. Caerwyn Williams and P.K. Ford, **The Irish Literary Tradition** (1992). This expanded English version of JECW's earlier **Traddodiad Llenyddol Iwerddon** (1958) incorporates the results of advances made during the intervening forty years, by scholars both from Ireland and from further afield. As kindred Celtic languages, Welsh and Irish possess traditional literatures which complement and illuminate each other at almost every point, and in spite of the major differences in the historical experiences of the two countries. This affinity is particularly evident in the earliest period, though it continues to be manifested throughout the Middle Ages, and in certain respects it persists even later. In early times Ireland and Wales possessed hierarchies of poets trained over a long period, who handed down the intricacies of their art from one generation to the next, in the composition of praise-poetry of considerable complexity. This was addressed to their kings and princes, and to the memory of the spiritual leaders of their two nations. Impressive examples of this verse have come down in Irish, as in Welsh, from as early as the sixth and seventh centuries. In addition to an ancient and distinguished tradition of poetry, originally preserved and transmitted orally, both Ireland and Wales evolved from early times a prose of great distinction, versatility and technical precision. This was adapted early in both countries to purposes as diverse as the recording of the native laws and technical

48

computations, together with a variegated and sophisticated narrative literature, which preserved relics from Celtic mythology and evoked remote memories of prehistoric events. Early Irish literature provides a commentary which cannot be disregarded for the light which it casts on the early literature and culture of Wales.

How to order publications

The inclusion of a title in this Guide does not imply that it is currently in print. To check availability, readers should consult *Whitakers Books in Print, Bookbank*, Book Data or write to the University of Wales Press for the latest catalogue. Further information is also available from the Press's Internet catalogue.

Orders may be placed with a bookseller or, in case of difficulty, sent direct to the University of Wales Press. Payment with order avoids the delays of *pro-forma* invoicing. Overseas payments are most easily made by credit card. The Press accepts Visa and Mastercard credit cards and Delta debit cards.

For details of agents in Australia and North America, please contact the Press.

University of Wales Press
6 Gwennyth Street
Cathays
Cardiff
CF2 4YD
Wales, UK
☎ +44(0)1222-231919
FAX +44(0)1222-230908
e-Mail: press@wales.ac.uk
URL   http://www.swan.ac.uk/uwp/home.htm